Write Yourself a
SUCCESSFUL
C.V.

Write Yourself a SUCCESSFUL C.V.

Get your career off to a winning start

Susan Stoyell

foulsham

LONDON · NEW YORK · TORONTO · SYDNEY

foulsham
Yeovil Road, Slough, Berkshire SL1 4JH

ISBN 0–572–01547–X
Copyright © 1989   Susan Stoyell

Printed in Great Britain by The Bath Press, Avon

CONTENTS

INTRODUCTION

YOU HAVE DECIDED THAT THE TIME IS RIGHT TO LEAVE THE ACADEMIC LIFE BEHIND YOU AND SET OUT IN YOUR WORKING CAREER. IT'S THE ROAD TO INDEPENDENCE.

Job hunting puts you through an active cycle of stages so we can take them in steps. First let us start by looking at an employer who has a vacancy for perhaps an apprentice electrician, a trainee computer operator, a junior secretary or a graduate electronics engineer. He has an opportunity for someone looking for their first job. What is he looking for in the applicants who apply?

ALWAYS IT WILL BE THE LEVEL OF KNOWLEDGE REQUIRED TO DO THE JOB AND A RECOGNISABLE 'POTENTIAL' THAT CAN BE DEVELOPED.

You have the potential. There is no doubt about that. And as we go step-by-step through this book the answers to the following questions will become clearer:

WHAT KIND OF POTENTIAL HAVE I?

HOW CAN I USE IT?

HOW WOULD I LIKE TO USE IT?

HOW CAN I DEMONSTRATE IT?

This is the beginning of a whole new life style for you. To put yourself on the right road there is a lot to think about, find out about and do — so let's make a start.

STEP 1
ESTABLISH A SENSE OF DIRECTION

OPPORTUNITIES — OPTIONS — Hold on a bit!

First think about your life to date. The subjects in which you have achieved your best results, the school, college/university activities that you have most enjoyed plus your achievements and enjoyments outside your academic environment.

Ask yourself: What am I likely to be most qualified to do? Which are my most marketable qualities? What kind of potential is it that I possess and how would I like to use it?

TAKE A LOOK AT YOURSELF

Form a picture of yourself as a whole and quite individual person. To help you find out about yourself try putting your ideas and conclusions down on paper. Let's look at four basic headings:

MY BEST SUBJECTS

THINGS I KNOW I LIKE FROM EXPERIENCE

WHAT'S IMPORTANT TO ME?

HOW DO I RATE MYSELF?

MY BEST SUBJECTS

List examination results (best grades first)

EXAM	GRADE

List examinations to be taken

EXAM	ESTIMATED GRADE

Awards/Certificates for non-academic achievements

e.g. Sports trophies Driving licence etc.

Here are some questions to ask yourself under the next two headings. Mark each with a tick, cross or question mark and add to the list any statements about yourself relevant to the heading.

THINGS I KNOW I LIKE FROM EXPERIENCE

√	X	?	
			Taking responsibility
			Using my organising ability
			Being in a team
			Leading a team
			Working/competing against time
			Being outside most of the time

√	X	?	
			Being inside most of the time
			Learning new skills
			Being in a large group or class
			Being in a small group or class
			Problem-solving activities or subjects
			Creative subjects or activities
			Practical/technical ('hands-on') subjects or activities
			Helping older people
			Helping younger people
			Studying
			Reading facts
			Reading fiction
			Being entertained
			Entertaining others
			Socialising with school/college friends
			Meeting new people
			Being with the family
			Dancing
			Listening to music
			Playing an instrument
			Singing
			Debating current affairs

✓	X	?	
			Reading national newspapers
			Watching the news on TV
			Watching TV documentaries
			Managing my money
			Dressing smartly most of the time
			Dressing smartly some of the time
			Dressing smartly none of the time
			Travelling
			Driving

WHAT'S IMPORTANT TO ME?

✓	X	?	
			Job satisfaction
			Job security
			A variety of duties
			Routine
			Opportunities for further training
			Opportunities for promotion
			Comfortable working environment
			Travelling distance to work
			Specific products/services that interest me
			Good starting salary

√	X	?	
			A large company
			A small company
			Social club
			Sports amenities
			Working with mostly young people
			Working with a mix of age groups

HOW DO I RATE MYSELF?

Try an honest personal rating of your abilities and score 0–10.

0	=	Poor or no experience
1–3	=	Quite good
4–6	=	Good
7–9	=	Very good
10	=	Excellent

	Practical/Technical ('hands on') skills
	Creative ability
	Analytical ability
	Organising ability
	Communication ability (oral)
	Communication ability (written)
	Working within a team
	Leading others

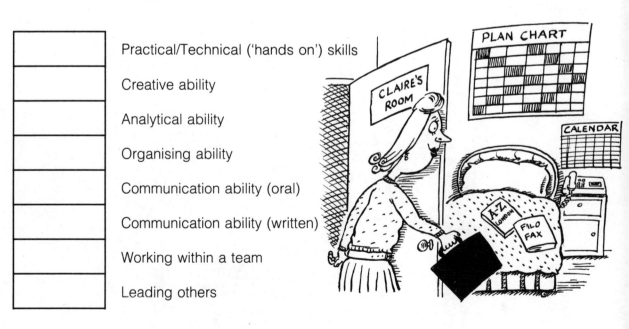

	Organising myself
	Adaptability
	Concentration
	Learning new skills

TALK OVER THE RESULTS

Now you have completed these exercises, take a sheet of paper and list:

1. *My best subjects*

2. *Things I know I like from experience* — list the positives that you have ticked.

3. *What's important to me?* — list the positives you have ticked.

4. *How do I rate myself?* — list in order your Excellent, Very Good and Good ratings.

Discuss this profile with people who know you well — your parents, your friends, your career advisers.

From these results you should now be forming a clearer picture of your strengths, interests and ambitions — with some interesting career ideas emerging in your mind.

So let's take it to the next step and see where and how you can find out more about your career options.

STEP 2
IT'S INFORMATION YOU NEED NOW

There is a tremendous amount of information available and sources of help when it comes to deciding which career is going to suit you — and you can't start getting it together too soon.

The first people to talk to are:

YOUR CAREERS TEACHER

YOUR CAREERS OFFICER

YOUR COLLEGE OR UNIVERSITY CAREERS ADVISERS

From these sources you will find some ideas and insight into the work and academic qualifications required in the careers that are of possible interest to you. They will be able to tell you some of your options — how and where your potential can be used.

There are other sources of information available as well, the most useful being:

PUBLIC LIBRARIES

You will find masses of careers information in the Lending and Reference sections.

BOOKSHOPS

You may want to buy some books that you feel are particularly useful. Get together with some friends who are looking at the job market and share the cost. Don't be afraid to ask the bookshop staff for help.

LOCAL AND NATIONAL NEWSPAPERS

Study the 'Situations Vacant' columns and cut out any advertisements that look interesting, even if it's not the time to put in applications. You may also find feature articles on particular companies or industries that appeal to you. All this information can be used later when you get to the application stage.

PERIODICALS AND TRADE PAPERS

This is another way to get a 'feel' for an industry that interests you and the career opportunities it offers. You will find many such specialist publications available at your library.

DIRECTORIES

These are useful sources of information if you are writing speculatively to companies. Writing 'on spec.' means applying for a vacancy when the company or organisation is not actually advertising for anyone. Try:

KOMPASS DIRECTORIES

These are particularly useful as they cover the UK and give detailed information on the companies listed, the location of which are clearly divided into counties and towns.

LOCAL DIRECTORIES

You will usually find that a local directory or list of local companies is available from your Library or Council offices.

YELLOW PAGES

The most obvious of all, especially if you are looking for a local job, as you probably have a copy at home.

TALKING TO PEOPLE

Relatives and friends are usually only too pleased to add to your careers information bank. Find out what they do and how they feel about their work. Do they have any contacts in the industries that you are considering?

BE BUSINESSLIKE IN THE WAY YOU COMPILE AND KEEP INFORMATION. START A FOLDER WHERE YOU CAN KEEP YOUR PERSONAL PROFILE, ALL YOUR ADVERTISE-MENTS, PRESS CUTTINGS AND NOTES.

CHECKLIST

Are you talking to: CAREERS TEACHER/ADVISER

CAREERS OFFICER

RELATIVES

FRIENDS

Are you looking at: LOCAL PAPERS

NATIONAL NEWSPAPERS

PERIODICALS/TRADE JOURNALS

CAREERS BOOKS

DIRECTORIES

Have you started : A CAREERS FOLDER

Having compiled a lot of information on your options, keep your mind clear by writing down, in order of preference, the careers that interest you most.

Referring back to your 'Personal Profile', I hope you are finding that your qualifications, strengths, likes and ambitions are matching up to the probable requirements of the kind of job you are looking for.

If you have a problem relating and matching them, now is the time to re-think and explore other career possibilities. This can save you venturing up some blind alleys. Remember: you will always have the potential that some employers will want.

STEP 3
YOUR PERSONAL MARKETING CAMPAIGN

You now have a file full of career facts, a list of attractive possible careers and a realistic self appraisal. Now's the time to demonstrate your potential, so let's get your personal marketing campaign together and show them what you have to offer.

THE C.V. (CURRICULUM VITAE — CAREER DETAILS)

Do it next — Do it now — It is worth doing well. A good C.V. is important. It is the first exhibit in your personal marketing campaign and whether the application lives on to the next stage and to an interview can depend on it.

A C.V. needs to give the facts about you in a clear and presentable way, so it captures and holds the interest of the reader and makes him want to meet you.

GUIDELINES TO WRITING A C.V.

Divide it into sections under separate headings. Some are a must whilst others are only useful if they are relevant to you. Suggested headings are (those marked with an * are a must for everyone including graduates. Those marked with an ˣ are a must for graduates and others to whom they are applicable):

Page 1

- * Personal details
- * Education
- ˣ Qualifications
- ˣ Non-academic achievements

* Responsibilities and offices held at school, college, university
* Leisure interests
* Work experience
* Career objectives
* Referees

Page 2

* Synopsis of degree course

A C.V. is better typed and kept short — one page if possible — unless you are a graduate and have a synopsis of the content of your degree course to include. If this is the case, the synopsis can stand alone on page 2.

SUGGESTED C.V. LAYOUT

PERSONAL DETAILS

Name:

Address:

Tel. No.:

Date of Birth/Age:

Nationality:

Marital Status:

Health:

Driving Licence:

EDUCATION

QUALIFICATIONS

NON-ACADEMIC ACHIEVEMENTS

RESPONSIBILITIES/OFFICES HELD AT SCHOOL/COLLEGE/UNIVERSITY

LEISURE INTERESTS

WORK EXPERIENCE

CAREER OBJECTIVES

REFEREES

N.B. If you are a graduate with a summary of your degree course to include, do so on a separate attached sheet.

NOTES ABOUT C.V. HEADINGS

PERSONAL DETAILS

NAME:
Give your first names in front of your surname, e.g. Janet Amanda Jones.

ADDRESS:
Give your full address and include the postcode.

TEL. NO.:
If you have a telephone number give it and indicate if you can be contacted during the day or evenings only; e.g. 01-000-1111 (evenings only).

DATE OF BIRTH/AGE:
Simple form, e.g. 25.10.70, followed by age in brackets.

NATIONALITY:
Give nationality, not country of birth; e.g. British (not English, Irish, Scottish, Welsh).

MARITAL STATUS:
Give Single or Married.

HEALTH:
If you are in good health give a full description; e.g. Good — I have suffered no serious illnesses or injuries and I am undergoing no medical treatment at this time.
If you are disabled or suffering from an illness requiring long-term medication then give brief details.
It is not necessary to give details of past illnesses from which you have completely recovered.

DRIVING LICENCE:
Give type of licence, e.g. Full, Provisional, Motor Cycle. If clean state clean. If you own a vehicle, then say so afterwards in brackets.

EDUCATION

Give schools, colleges, polytechnic or university.
Give dates, name of school, college, polytechnic, university and address. For example:

1979–1983   SOMETHING SECONDARY SCHOOL,
High Street, Middlewitch, Nr. Sandwich, Surrey

1983–1985   SOMETHING SIXTH FORM COLLEGE,
High Street, High Town, Surrey

1985–1988   SOMETHING POLYTECHNIC,
King Street, Newtown, Kent

QUALIFICATIONS

List examinations taken and passed and those where you are awaiting results. Give highest grades first.

SUBJECT   *GRADE*

SUBJECT   *ESTIMATED GRADE* (AWAITING RESULT)

Note: Do not supply some grades and not others. If the grades are not good leave them out in all cases and just give subjects passed.

NON-ACADEMIC ACHIEVEMENTS

Give those where you have achieved a certificate, a trophy, or an award of some kind. For instance:

Sporting: certificate for swimming
green belt for judo
Dancing: bronze/silver/gold medal
Other   :   Duke of Edinburgh bronze/silver/gold medal

RESPONSIBILITIES/OFFICES HELD AT SCHOOL/COLLEGE/UNIVERSITY

Give those that show you have been put in a position of trust or responsibility. For instance:

Captain of the First Eleven Cricket Team
Treasurer of Chess Club
Chairman of Debating Society

Remember: Avoid anything that shows a strong party political bias, unless, of course, you are looking for a career in politics.

LEISURE INTERESTS

Give four or five of your favourite hobbies and try and find a good mix showing you in a switched on and switched off mode. Strike a good balance between the physically active and more intellectual pursuits. Do not bluff, however, and put something down that you know little about — you could easily be caught out if asked to elaborate at an interview. An example of a good mix would be:

Playing cricket

Playing squash

Listening to music (giving type: jazz, pop or classical)

Active member of a conservation society

Philately

WORK EXPERIENCE

Give details of any work experience — when it was, where it was and what it was. For instance:

1987 (Summer holidays)	J.C. Smith and Sons.	Packer
1988 (Christmas holidays)	The Post Office	Post sorter

CAREER OBJECTIVES

Go back to your self-assessment exercises in Step 1 and look at 'What's Important to Me?' If you have been quite specific about the type of job environment you are looking for then be precise in your given objectives. If you want to keep your options open and apply for several different types of job, then keep it vague or leave out this section.

Example of the specific   I feel that I have the potential to develop a successful career in accountancy and I would like to work for a company that can offer me the necessary breadth of opportunity and I hope the assistance to further my studies towards a professional qualification.

Example of the non-specific   I am keen to find a progressive position with a company that can offer me training and the scope to develop a successful career.

REFEREES

Give two referees. One could be the Head of your last school or college. The other should be a personal referee — if possible someone who holds a position of authority and status and who knows you quite well. Perhaps someone who has employed you during weekend or holiday periods might be ideal. *Important*: Do not forget to ask them first if they mind being given as a referee.

A PHOTOGRAPH — IS IT A GOOD IDEA?

Quite simply 'Yes' if you are applying for jobs where appearance is likely to be of particular importance. If you cannot find room on your C.V., then affix it to your Application Letter. A head and shoulders is best and black and white all that is necessary.

CHECKLIST ON YOUR C.V.

Look at your draft and compare it against the examples given here. Does it contain the four essentials:

> PERSONAL DETAILS
>
> EDUCATION
>
> LEISURE INTERESTS
>
> REFEREES

Is it on A4 paper?
Is it the right length?
Are the dates you have given correct?
Have you asked your chosen referees if they are agreeable?
Have you checked the spelling?

If you are happy you could now get it typed — and do not forget to ask someone else to check the final article.

Now you are all set to have it photocopied (most post offices and libraries have this facility available).

Store your C.V.s somewhere where they can be kept flat, crisp and clean.

C.V. EXAMPLES

On pages 24–28 are examples of five C.V.s in which the applicants are marketing themselves to take full advantage of their individual qualifications, achievements, and career objectives. These are the kinds of C.V. that will make the reader want to meet you!

Name:	Deborah FREEMAN
Address:	12 Woodpecker Lane, London W1 3BA
Tel. No.:	01-000-000 (evenings)
Date of birth:	12.2.67 (age 22)
Nationality:	British
Marital status:	Single
Health:	Good — I have suffered no serious illness or injury and I am not receiving any medical treatment at this time
Driving licence:	Full/clean (car/motor cycle owner)

EDUCATION

1978–1983:	SOMETHING SECONDARY SCHOOL, London W1
1983–1985:	SOMETHING SIXTH FORM COLLEGE, London W1
1985–1988:	UNIVERSITY OF SOMETHING, London W1

QUALIFICATIONS

GCE 'O' Levels:	Mathematics (A), Technical Drawing (A), Physics (B), Chemistry (B), Geography (B), English Language (C), French (C)
'A' Levels	Physics (A), Mathematics (A), Chemistry (B)
Degree Course	Final Year of 3-year degree course Engineering Science.

NON-ACADEMIC ACHIEVEMENTS

St. John's Ambulance First Aid Certificate

RESPONSIBILITIES/OFFICES HELD AT SCHOOL/COLLEGE/UNIVERSITY

Member of Fund-raising Committee
Stage Manager of Last Rag Review
Captain of College First Hockey Team

LEISURE INTERESTS

Squash, Theatre, Music (Jazz), Computing

WORK EXPERIENCE

Summer 1985	Farm	Fruit picker
Winter 1985	Post Office	Postal worker
Summer 1986	G. Armitage	VDU clerk (Purchasing)
Winter 1986	G. Armitage	Stock controller

CAREER OBJECTIVES

I see myself as a flexible, practical person who has been trained in analytical methods and I would like to utilise this training within an Engineering/Project Management environment.

REFEREES

Dr. R. Hill,	Mr. G. Townsend,
Engineering Department,	Managing Director,
Something University,	G. Armitage & Co.,
Something Town,	Finbow Street,
Something County	London W1

N.B. Please see details of my degree course attached.

CURRICULUM VITAE: Example 2

Name:	Janet ROWLAND
Address:	Field Gate, High View, Tipton, Sussex SS1 1SS
Tel. No.:	0000-0000 (evenings)
Date of birth:	20.1.70 (age 19)
Nationality:	British
Marital status:	Single
Health:	Good — I have suffered no serious illness or injury and I am not receiving any medical treatment at this time
Driving licence:	Full/clean (I intend buying a car when I start work)

EDUCATION

1981–1986:	TORINGTON SCHOOL, Torington, Sussex
1986–1988:	SOMETHING COLLEGE, New Town, Sussex

QUALIFICATIONS

GCE 'O' Levels:	English Language (A), Biology (B), Mathematics (B), Chemistry (C), French (C)
RSA (1):	Typing
'A' Levels	Subjects taken with estimated grades: English (B), Geography (C)

NON-ACADEMIC ACHIEVEMENTS

Current holder of the Something Show Jumping Championship

LEISURE INTERESTS

Member of College Conservation Society
Swimming, Disco Dancing, Reading

WORK EXPERIENCE

Summer 1987	Daily Chronicle, Torington, Sussex	Messenger
Winter 1987	Moat Hotel, Torington, Sussex	Kitchen Assistant

CAREER OBJECTIVES

I am looking for an opportunity to work in a sales office where I would be trained in general office procedure, come to understand the company's products and eventually be trained for a career in field sales.

REFEREES

Mr. C. Penn,	Mr. B. Thorpe,
Headmaster,	Editor,
Something College,	Daily Chronicle,
New Town,	Torington,
Sussex	Sussex

CURRICULUM VITAE: Example 3

Name:	Matthew Gareth EVANS
Address:	1 Valley Way, Caernarfon, Gwynedd, GW2 5KB
Tel. No.:	0000-00000 (evenings)
Date of birth:	12.5.73 (age 16)
Nationality:	British
Marital status:	Single
Health:	Good. I have suffered no serious illness or injury and I am not receiving medical treatment at this time.
Driving licence:	Provisional Group E (Moped)

EDUCATION

1985–1989:   SOMETHING SCHOOL, CAERNARFON

QUALIFICATIONS

GCSE Exams	Awaiting Results — Estimated Grades
Technical Drawing	(B)
Mathematics	(C)
Biology	(C)
Physics	(C)
English Language	(C/D)

NON-ACADEMIC ACHIEVEMENTS

Played in school football team. Have taken part in various fund raising charity walks and swims.

RESPONSIBILITIES/OFFICES HELD AT
SCHOOL/COLLEGE

First-year prefect

LEISURE INTERESTS:

Car Mechanics, Playing Football, Design/Build Model Aeroplanes

DETAILS OF WORK EXPERIENCE

Summer 1988
to date: Something Newsagents   Newspaper Round

CAREER OBJECTIVES

I am a practical person and would like to learn a trade. After serving an apprenticeship and having gained good experience I would hope to have started my own business once I have reached thirty years of age.

REFEREES:

Mr. J. King,	Mrs. S. Davies
Headmaster,	Manager,
Something School,	Something Newsagents,
Caernarfon,	Caernarfon,
Gwynned GW16 9JU	Gwynned GW1 2JR

CURRICULUM VITAE: Example 4

Name:	Jishno RAO
Address:	12 King Street, New Town, Lancs., MK20 2JB
Tel. No.:	000-00000 (evenings)
	111-11111 (days)
Date of birth:	20.2.71 (age 18)
Nationality:	British
Marital status:	Single
Health:	Good. I have suffered no serious illness or injury and I am not receiving medical treatment at this time.
Driving licence:	Full/clean (car owner)

EDUCATION

1983–1987:	SOMETHING SCHOOL, New Town
1987–1989:	SOMETHING COLLEGE, New Town

QUALIFICATIONS:

GCSE — English Literature (B)
   Geography (B)
   English Language (C)
   Mathematics (C)
   Biology (C)
   Chemistry (D)
Hotel & Catering Operations
BTec National Diploma

NON-ACADEMIC ACHIEVEMENTS

Duke of Edinburgh Award (Bronze)

RESPONSIBILITIES/OFFICES HELD

AT SCHOOL/COLLEGE

Captain First Eleven School Cricket Team

LEISURE INTERESTS:

Playing Cricket, Reading, Chess

WORK EXPERIENCE

Spring 1988	The Bridge Hotel	Waiter
Winter 1988	The Bridge Hotel	Waiter
Summer 1987	The Swan Hotel	Kitchen Hand
Winter 1987	The Bridge Hotel	Kitchen Hand/ Vegetable Chef

CAREER OBJECTIVES

I have enjoyed my BTec course and have done well. I hope to find a position as Trainee Manager in a hotel which is part of a major group where opportunity exists for successful trainees to make rapid career progress.

REFEREES:

Mr. S. Johnson	Mr. C. Richards
Headmaster,	The Manager,
Something College	The Bridge Hotel,
New Town,	New Town,
Lancs. MK25 7ST	Lancs. MK20 5ET

CURRICULUM VITAE: Example 5

Name:	Jonathon Peter KIRBY
Address:	The Farm, River Lane, Switcham, Norfolk, IP23 6JD
Tel. No.:	0000-00000 (days/evenings)
Date of birth:	6.6.73 (age 16)
Nationality:	British
Marital status:	Single
Weight:*	85 lbs.
Health:	Good. I have suffered no serious illness or injury and I am not receiving any medical treatment at this time.
Driving Licence:	Full/clean Group E (Moped)

EDUCATION

1985–1989:   SOMETHING SCHOOL, Switcham

QUALIFICATIONS:

GCSE: Biology (C)
English Language (C)
Mathematics (C)

NON-ACADEMIC ACHIEVEMENTS

Have won a number of inter-school swimming championships.

RESPONSIBILITIES/OFFICES
HELD AT SCHOOL

Prefect

LEISURE INTERESTS: Horses, following the racing news, mountaineering

WORK EXPERIENCE

1986 to date	Something Newsagents	Morning Paper Round
Summer 1987	Something Riding School	Stable Hand
Winter 1988	Something Riding School	Stable Hand

CAREER OBJECTIVES

I am competitive and mentally and physically strong. I would like to be apprentice to a successful National Hunt Stables and prove myself a winning jockey with the ultimate ambition of winning the Grand National at least once in my career.

REFEREES:	Mr. S. Thomas,	Captain R. Wainwright,
	Something School,	Something Stables,
	Switcham,	Newtown,
	Norfolk IP24 7LN	Norfolk IP20 2NU

*See special addition — 'weight'. If you have thought the career through you will realise this is an important piece of information.

COMPANY APPLICATION FORMS

Care counts for a lot so . . . Get it right!

Most companies have application forms. On them, you sign a declaration that the facts you have given about yourself are correct and, used in the early stages, the interview shortlist is usually decided from the information they provide.

You may find that in an advertisement, you are asked to telephone in or write for a company application form. Do as you are asked but clip your C.V. to it.

Or you might be given one to complete just before your interview, just after your interview, at the second interview stage or even just prior to an offer. It depends on a company's recruitment procedure and there are no hard and fast rules that apply.

At whichever point you have to complete such a form, always tackle it carefully. The degree of care you show in undertaking this sometimes tedious task tells the reader much about you.

Complete it in black ink (it reproduces better if it has to be photocopied) using a good pen or ball pen and avoid crossings out or smudges. If you are doing it at home or off the company premises, make sure you have a flat clean surface on which to write.

Read the form well first — as you would an exam paper — and think out your answers before putting pen to paper. Usually you will be instructed to use BLOCK CAPITALS — make sure you do and from beginning to end. The form will usually ask you to give your SURNAME IN A SEPARATE BOX TO YOUR FIRST NAMES. The SURNAME more often than not comes first with Mr. Mrs. Ms. Miss printed alongside — cross out whichever three are not applicable in your case.

It will look something like this:

SURNAME: Mr.Mrs.Ms.Miss Please use BLOCK CAPITALS	FIRST NAMES:

Remember to have your C.V. with you at all times when you could be asked to complete an application form. It makes life a lot easier for you as contained in it you will have the kind of detailed factual information you do not necessarily carry in your head, all ready, checked and correct, covering qualification gradings and dates.

Some company forms can be quite long and complicated. If there are questions that you do not understand ask someone to explain after you have completed what you can.

Do not leave questions unanswered if they do not apply to you. Simply state N/A, this means 'not applicable'. By doing this, the reader can see that you have not left out anything by mistake.

There are certain questions that you will come across that could do with clarifying. For instance:

CHRISTIAN NAMES: Same as first names or forenames

SURNAME:	This is your last name or family name
SOURCE OF APPLICATION:	They want to know how you heard about the vacancy. If it was a newspaper advert, state which paper and the date the advert appeared.
NEXT OF KIN:	They want to know the name, and sometimes the address as well, of the person most closely related to you. If you are unmarried it is likely to be your father, mother or guardian. If you are married, it will be your husband or wife.
DEPENDANTS:	They want to know if there are people that you are actually responsible for, such as children.

APPLICATION FORM CHECKLIST

Have you read the form carefully?
Do you understand all the questions?
Have you noted special instructions like using BLOCK CAPITALS?
Have you noted which order to enter your names?
Do you have a good pen/ball point?
Are dates/grades given consistent with those on your C.V.?
Have you thought out an answer to all questions?
Have you a flat, clean surface on which to write?

COMPLETING AN APPLICATION FORM — RIGHT AND WRONG

Here are a couple of examples of completed application forms. In Example 1 (page 31), James has made a good job of completing the form clearly and fully.

Example 2 (page 32), however, is a different story and it contains some basic and commonly made mistakes. Can you spot them? There are ten in all. You can check them with the answers provided below.

1. Under SURNAME: has not used BLOCK CAPITALS.

2. Under FIRST NAME(S): has put FIRST NAMES IN SURNAME BOX.

3. Under ADDRESS: has not put the postal code.

4. Under DATE OF BIRTH: has put current year instead of year of birth.

5. Under PLACE OF BIRTH: should be *Gimchurch, Middlesex.*

6. Under NATIONALITY: should be *BRITISH.*

7. Under HEALTH: has left blank.

8. Under LEISURE INTERESTS: *Football* spelt wrongly.

9. Under NEXT OF KIN: relationship should be *Father.*

10. Under QUALIFICATIONS: has omitted Biology grade.

EXAMPLE I: COMPLETED APPLICATION — THE RIGHT WAY

BLOGGS AND BLOGGS LIMITED

PLEASE RETURN THIS APPLICATION FORM TO:

ANSWER IN BLOCK CAPITALS

THE PERSONNEL DEPT.,
BLOGGS AND BLOGGS LTD.,
GIMCHURCH,
MIDDLESEX

CONFIDENTIAL   APPLICATION FOR EMPLOYMENT

Source of application THE DAILY CHRONICLE 18/6/89 Date of application 20·6·89

Post applied for JUNIOR ACCOUNTS CLERK (REF. A/JiC)

Surname: Mr.Mrs.Miss.Ms. BROWN	First Name(s): JAMES MICHAEL
Address: 25, THE MOOR, GIMCHURCH, MIDDLESEX MX2 ILE	Telephone Number(s): 000 - 0000

Date of Birth: 1 1 70	Place of Birth: HARROW MIDDX	Nationality: BRITISH
Marital Status: SINGLE	Ages of Children: N/A	

Details of Disabilities or Serious Illnesses: NONE

Do You Hold: A current Driving Licence (Class): NO	Details of any Endorsements: N/A
Do You Own: A House NO	A Car NO	

Leisure Activities: PLAYING FOOTBALL, ORNITHOLOGY, CINEMA

NEXT OF KIN

Surname Mr.Mrs.Miss.Ms. BROWN First Name(s) JOHN JAMES Relationship FATHER

Address: 25, THE MOOR, GIMCHURCH, MIDDLESEX MX2 ILE	Telephone Number(s): 000 - 0000

Education: Schools, Colleges, Polytechnics, Universities:

GIMCHURCH SCHOOL, GIMCHURCH, MIDDX

BLANK TECHNICAL COLLEGE, FINSTONE, MIDDX

Qualifications: GCSE: ENGLISH LANG (A) MATHS (A) GEOGRAPHY (B)
FRENCH (C) BIOLOGY (C)

'A' LEVELS TAKEN - AWAITING RESULTS.
MATHS, APPLIED MATHS, GEOGRAPHY.

Referees: Give Names and Addresses MR. J. SMITH BLANK TECHNICAL COLLEGE, HIGHWAY, FINSTONE, MIDDX MX1 3JJ	MRS. J. STANDING 25, SOUTH VIEW, GIMCHURCH, MIDDX MX1 2PT

EXAMPLE 2: COMPLETED APPLICATION — THE WRONG WAY

BLOGGS AND BLOGGS LIMITED

PLEASE RETURN THIS APPLICATION FORM TO:

ANSWER IN BLOCK CAPITALS

THE PERSONNEL DEPT.,
BLOGGS AND BLOGGS LTD.,
GIMCHURCH,
MIDDLESEX

CONFIDENTIAL   APPLICATION FOR EMPLOYMENT

Source of application *The Daily Chronicle 18/6/89* Date of application *20. 6. 89*
Post applied for *Junior Accounts Clerk*

Surname: Mr. Mrs. Miss. Ms. *James Micheal Smith*	First Name(s):
Address: *25, The Moor Gimchurch Middlesex*	Telephone Number(s): *000 - 0000*

Date of Birth: *1. 1. 89*	Place of Birth: *Hospital*	Nationality: *English*
Marital Status: *Single*	Ages of Children: *N/A*	

Details of Disabilities or Serious Illnesses:

Do You Hold: A current Driving Licence (Class): *No*	Details of any Endorsements:
Do You Own: A House *No*	A Car *No*	

Leisure Activities: *Playing Football*

NEXT OF KIN

Surname Mr. Mrs. Miss. Ms. *Brown* First Name(s) *John James* Relationship *Good.*
Address: Telephone Number(s):

Education: Schools, Colleges, Polytechnics, Universities:
Gimchurch School, Gimchurch, Middlesex
Blank Technical College, Finstone, Middlesex.

Qualifications: *GCSE*
English Languge (A) Maths (A) Geography (B)
French (C) Biology

Referees: Give Names and Addresses
Mr J. Smith
Blank Technical College
Highway, Finstone, Maldx MX35PP

Mrs J. Standing
25, South view
Gimchurch   Middx
HK12DT

32

APPLICATION LETTERS

Show them you have style . . .

A letter accompanying a C.V. can be brief but should be 'punchy'. Think about it and draft it out until you have it right. The points to remember are:

Use good quality plain A4 note paper

Use a good pen or ball point

Use black ink

Keep your lines straight

Watch your writing

Watch your grammar

Watch your spelling

Make a carbon or photocopy

Keep your application letters in a file clipped together with the original letter

The other points that are easy to forget but worth remembering are:

Your address should be written in full (remembering the post code) top right of the paper, followed by the date written in full.

Top left of paper you should put the name of the person or the title of the person to whom you have been asked to send the application, followed underneath by the name of the company and the address with below that any reference numbers given to you in the advertisement.

If you have been given the name of a person to whom the letter and application should be sent, start the letter: Dear Mr. Smith or whoever. If the recipient is a woman and it is not known whether she is a Mrs. or a Miss, use Ms., e.g. Dear Ms. Smith. When you are writing to a named person sign off: Yours sincerely, followed underneath by your own name. In situations where the person who will receive the letter is not named, use Dear Sir and sign the letter off: Yours faithfully, followed again by your own name.

Underneath your own signature it is a good idea to print your name.

Typical Application Letter Layout

12 The Avenue,
New Town,
Middlesex
MC2 1LX

Mr. L.C. Smith,
The Personnel Manager,
Wyvern Engineering Company Limited,
Saxon Industrial Estate,
New Town,
Middlesex
MC1 2QY

Ref. AC/221/J

20th July 1989

Dear Mr. Smith,

Re: Accounts Clerk. Your Advertisement: The Chronicle 19.7.89

Yours sincerely,

ANDREW FLETCHER

THE WORDS THAT GET THE COMPANY MESSAGE ACROSS

Replying to an advertisement, the right words will not come until you have read and re-read the advertisement and have broken down exactly what it is that has attracted you to the vacancy. Try doing it this way:

Underline in red the words that caught your eye. They might have been:

THE COMPANY NAME	It might be a company you know something about — perhaps it's a company in your careers file, you might know people there or they might be situated close to where you live
THE TYPE OF BUSINESS	Its products or services
THE JOB ITSELF	It could be just what you have in mind for yourself
THE COMPANY LOCATION	It might be situated close to you — or perhaps it offers transport by a company bus

Hopefully it will be a combination of several of these factors. Also, descriptive phrases might be important to you, such as:

an international company

a multi-million pound turnover

an expanding company

part of a major group of companies

offering excellent prospects

offering excellent training facilities

offering a clean working environment

the UK market leader in . . .

Underline in blue or black the specified requirements they are asking for that suit your abilities. They could be:

educated to . . . standard

an analytical mind

good communication skills

an interest in computers

a bright young person willing to train in . . .

aged . . . years

a smart appearance

THE WORDS THAT GET YOUR MESSAGE ACROSS

Now look back at your personal assessments and think about the job you are applying for — if and how you fit the bill and whether it satisfies your requirements. If you are clear on these points, the letter will not be a problem.

If all the signs are good, you will be feeling enthusiastic. So let's start writing.

SPELLING OUT YOUR POTENTIAL

Be Keen, Be Clear, Be Sincere.
The messages you need to get across are, 'I am keen, I am clear and I am sincere'.

FIRST PARAGRAPH: I am keen —

You are making the statement that you are keen on applying for the vacancy.

SECOND PARAGRAPH: *I am clear and understand what I have read* —

Show that you have read the advertisement carefully and have a good understanding of the job and the company requirements. Say why you think you match their requirements.

THIRD PARAGRAPH: *I am clear and businesslike*

Make it easier for the company by saying when you are available for interview and when you are available to start work. If you make these facts clear then it can save the company a lot of time making and re-making appointments to suit a number of people apart from yourself.

FOURTH PARAGRAPH: *I am sincere*

Round off the letter by leaving them in no doubt that you are sincerely interested in the job.

APPLICATION LETTER: EXAMPLE A

A nice little advert that tells you all you need to know — the job, what it involves, the type of company they are and the type of person they are looking for.

Advertisement: Example A

<u>JUNIOR ADMINISTRATOR</u>

A <u>smart</u>, <u>enthusiastic young</u> person is required to join our energetic <u>sales administration team</u>. You will be dealing with <u>customer enquiries</u> and orders mostly <u>taken by telephone</u>. <u>BLANK</u> store is one of a <u>multi-branch retail chain</u> specialising in <u>computers</u>. The <u>prospects are excellent</u> for an <u>ambitious</u> young person with <u>initiative</u> and an <u>interest in computers</u>. <u>Age 17–20</u> preferred. Apply in writing to . . .

I have underlined the points that most suitable applicants will find relevant and attractive. You might apply along these lines:

36

12 Sun Hill,
Uckthorpe,
Middlesex
MM2 0LJ

16 June 1989

Miss J. Smith,
Blank Store,
2, High Street,
Uckthorpe,
Middlesex
MM1 6QJ

Dear Miss Smith,

Re: Your vacancy for a Junior Administrator,
The Daily Chronicle 15.6.89.

I have read your advertisement for a Junior Administrator and I am keen to apply. Please find my C.V. enclosed.

This would seem an ideal opportunity to combine my interest in computers and my interest in a retailing career and I believe that I have what it takes to match your requirements.

I am 17 years old
I care about my appearance
I am enthusiastic
I work well in a team
I like using the telephone
I have a computer and have done some programming
I am ambitious
I like using my initiative

I leave school on 25 June and I would be available to start work immediately afterwards. If you wish to see me for an interview, I would be pleased to attend any day after 4.0 pm. or on a Saturday. After I have left school, I could come any time.

I hope that you will consider me a good candidate for the job.

Yours sincerely,

PAUL PAGE

keen: A good positive word

believe: Shows confidence in own judgement

ideal: Shows you are attaching importance to finding the 'right' job and not just any old job

hope: Re-enforces keeness and is a polite, nice way to round off the letter

APPLICATION LETTER: EXAMPLE B

This is a very short advert that tells you very little. Therefore there is little to pick up from it to use in your letter. Again I have underlined points you might find attractive but you will need to build on that information and add to it if you are to write a good letter of application.

Advertisement: Example B

BLANK HAIR SALON
JUNIOR
Required urgently to join
our team. Top wages paid
Apply in writing to . . .

What is the employer looking for when they sift through the applications? They are a hairdressing business looking for a junior urgently. These are the things you know, but what else? Try to look at the job through the employer's eyes and make some careful assumptions.

They are likely to be looking for:

someone with an interest in hair styling

a creative person

someone with a smart appearance

a hard-working person

someone who gets on well with people

You could apply along these lines:

10 Cedar Way,
Upten,
Gloucs
GL15 9JJ

13 June 1989

Mrs. J Brown,
Style Hair Salon,
5, King Street,
Upten,
Gloucs
GL20 6SU

Dear Mrs. Brown,

Re: Your vacancy for a Junior, The Daily Chronicle 12.6.89.

I have read your advertisement for a Junior and I am keen to apply. Please find my C.V. enclosed.

This vacancy seems an ideal opportunity to train with a local and well established hair salon and I believe that I could make a success with the job.

I enjoy styling my own hair and other people's
I care about my appearance
I get on well with people — all age groups
I am hard working
I could start work immediately

Having left school on the 28th May and just come back from holiday, I am hoping to find a job in hairdressing that I can start soon.

If you would like to interview me, I would be pleased to come and see you anytime except next Tuesday.

I hope that you will consider me for the vacancy.

Yours sincerely,

SHEILA WATSON

LETTER ASKING FOR AN APPLICATION FORM

You will sometimes be invited to write off for an application form. In these cases, a very brief letter is all that is needed — a longer letter should be sent when you return the application form.

You can write along these lines:

22 Orchard Drive,
Bedford,
MK41 2JG

17 August 1989

Miss P.J. Jones,
Personnel Manager,
Blank Electronics Company,
High View Estate,
Bedford,
MK25 6PL

Dear Miss Jones,

Re: Your vacancy for a Trainee Electronics Engineer,
    Daily Chronicle 16.8.89.

I would like to apply for the vacancy of Trainee Electronics Engineer with your company and I would be grateful if you would send me an application form.

Yours sincerely,

KATE BROWN

LETTER TO ACCOMPANY AN APPLICATION FORM

Let us go back to the letter in reply to our Example A Advertisement (page 37) and see how this particular application letter can be easily changed to accompany an application form. It is the first and last paragraphs that need altering — then it does the job well. These could now be written along the following lines:

Thank you for sending me the application form which I have completed and have pleasure in returning to you together with my C.V.

I leave school on the 29th June and I could be available to start work immediately afterwards. If you wish to see me for an interview, I would be pleased to attend any day after 4.0 pm or earlier in the day if two days notice is given.

SPECULATIVE APPLICATIONS

When you find a company that you might like to work for, although you do not have any particular reason for thinking that they have a suitable opening, it is worth a speculative approach to them — provided you are prepared for disappointment. Having said that, it is surprising how often these longer shots pay off.

Whether a company has a vacancy to fill or not, they are attracted to a speculative approach because it demonstrates *energy, courage and enthusiasm in the applicant.*

MAKING THE FIRST MOVE

So you're making the first move and applying to a company in the hope that they will have a position to suit you. The most important thing is to send your letter to a named person. That way you can be sure that the letter will attract serious attention and draw a response. Telephone the company and ask the telephonist for the name and initials of their Personnel Manager. If they do not have a Personnel Manager, ask for the name of the Manager of the department that is of interest to you.

For instance, if you are wanting a job as a Trainee Computer Operator you need the name of the Data Processing Manager. If you are interested in a Marketing job then you need the name of the Marketing Manager, and so forth. Perhaps you are applying for a secretarial or clerical position that is not allied to any particular department. The Company Secretary might well be your answer in this situation.

Speculative letters should be brief, spelling out why you are interested in the company, giving your qualifications and skills and any qualities which you think may be of interest to them. Accompany the letter with your C.V.

You may find some companies keep your letter on file for a few weeks in case a suitable vacancy occurs so you might not hear anything for quite a long period of time. You may not hear from them at all in fact. Don't let this discourage you or put you off applying to their advertisements in the future. It may simply mean that their system does not cope well with speculative applications and, to be fair, they probably receive a lot. However, if you don't get any response it is safe to assume that there is nothing suitable for you at the moment.

A speculative letter should be written along these lines:

12 Sun Hill,
Bedford,
MK22 6JJ

Mr. P.J. Jones,   20 June 1989
Personnel Manager
Blank Electronics Company Limited,
High View Industrial Estate,
Bedford
MK25 6PL

Dear Mr. Jones,

I am writing to you with my C.V. enclosed in the hope that you may have a vacancy for a Trainee Electronics Technician.

My qualifications to date are 6 good GCSE passes and I am about to take Physics, Chemistry and Maths 'A' Levels.

I am very keen on Electronics and read as much as possible on the subject by visiting the Reference Library and looking at Trade Journals such as Electronics Weekly and Electronics Times. In my leisure time I enjoy using my computer and have done some programming in BASIC.

If you have a vacancy that might suit me, I would be very pleased to have the opportunity of an interview and could attend any day except for the week commencing 26th June. I would be able to start work after 20th July.

I hope that this application will be of interest to you.

Yours sincerely,

JOHN SMITH

CHECK IT!

The examples I have given of application letters are intended as guides only and have been provided to give you 'a feel' of how they should be approached. Remember, though, that a good application is a reflection of you, so find your own words and let your enthusiasm and personality shine through.

Keep a copy of each letter you write, clip it to the advertisement to which you are applying, and keep them in a separate folder file. Make it your APPLICATION FILE.

A habit you should get into before writing to a prospective employer is to go through the following checks:

Is it on good quality A4 paper?

Have you used a good pen/ball pen?

Have you used black ink?

Is your writing neat?

Are the lines straight?

Are the grammar and spelling correct?

Does it put the message across?

Have you enclosed your C.V.?

Have you made a copy?

Have you clipped the copy of your letter to the original advertisement?

Have you started an application file?

TELEPHONE REPLIES

When you apply for a job in response to an advertisement, sometimes you are invited to telephone for an application form or appointment. Sometimes you are given the option of telephoning or writing.

If you are given either option, I recommend telephoning if possible because it shows enthusiasm and confidence. It's a way you can chalk up some plus points at a very early stage. Not only that, there is less chance that the job will be filled by someone else who reacts more quickly than you and has the offer of the job perhaps before your application has had time to reach the company.

If possible use a private telephone and ensure you have enough space to take notes and make the call where you can be relaxed and undisturbed. If you are using a telephone box, be sure that you have enough money or units on your Phonecard for quite a long call.

Listen carefully to what is being asked of you. Speak clearly and not too quickly. Keep your answers brief and to the point. Avoid asking any more questions than are necessary. Your time to ask questions will come at the face-to-face interview.

TELEPHONING FOR AN APPOINTMENT

If you are invited to telephone for an appointment and not given the option to write, you can be fairly sure that the conversation will involve a short interview.

Have the advertisement in front of you with all the points underlined that have attracted you to the job and the specified requirements that you match.
Have your C.V. in front of you
Have a diary in front of you
Have a note pad with written notes to act as memory-joggers. The notes will include headings such as these:

Date of call:

Company:

Telephone No.:

Name of person you have been asked to call:

Extension number of person you have been asked to call:

The Job Title:

Where the vacancy was advertised:

Appointment: Day . . . . Date . . . . Time . . . .

The name of the person you are to ask for on arrival:

The address where the inverview is to be held:

Any directions on how to find the company:

BEFORE YOU HANG UP MAKE SURE:

1. That the company has your name, address and telephone number.

2. That you have repeated the day, date and time of the interview.

ADDITIONAL NOTES

Questions about the following may arise in the conversation:

Why the job is interesting to you (look at your underlinings on the advertisement — pick up the points)

    1.

    2.

    3.

    4.

Why the job is suitable for you (look at your underlinings on the advertisement — pick up the points)

    1.

    2.

    3.

    4.

TELEPHONING FOR AN APPLICATION FORM

This is likely to be a quick call to the person named in the advertisement. You should give your name, address, telephone number (if you are on the 'phone), and the vacancy for which you are applying. It is probable that no further questions will be asked of you but be fully prepared just in case. You could find that the telephone call takes on the form of a short interview, so make your notes as suggested before in 'Telephoning for an Appointment'.

CHECKLIST — BEFORE YOU PICK UP THE PHONE

Have you made your notes?

Do you have a note pad?

Do you have a pen (which is working)?

If calling from a box, do you have enough money or Phonecard units?

Do you have the advert?

Do you have your C.V.?

Do you have a diary?

Have you worked out exactly what you are going to say when your call is answered?

GET IN TOUCH — KEEP YOUR APPLICATIONS ALIVE

Regularly refer to your Application File and, where you find that you have applied for a specific vacancy and have not heard from the company after a couple of weeks or so from writing or returning an application form, it is a good idea to phone them and speak to the person to whom you applied. Ask them politely if they have any news or when they expect that there might be news for you. This kind of follow-up, approached in the right manner and spirit, can go down well. It serves as an indicator of your serious interest in the vacancy but NEVER MAKE YOUR CONTACT FEEL THAT YOU ARE PRESSURISING THEM.

After all this initial effort, you will have made several applications and I feel sure that by now you are logging some appointments into your diary.

Things are happening and the signs are that the effort is proving worthwhile.

STEP 4
THE INTERVIEW

THE DAY BEFORE — It's countdown time

PUT EVERYTHING TOGETHER

Collate everything that you will need for the interview and transfer it all to a separate file/bag/case. If you are using your old school bag or case, make sure it's in good condition. Do not use a plastic carrier bag.

CHECKLIST

Make sure that you have:

The original advert

Your C.V.

A copy of the application letter

Your telephone notes

Your letter asking you to attend the interview

The job description (if provided with one)

Company literature/information (that you have compiled or they have sent to you)

Copies of your examination certificates

Maps/timetables/directions on how to get there

A note of the name of the person to ask for when you arrive

The company address and telephone number

Two pens

A note pad (with your memory-jogger notes)

MEMORY-JOGGERS

Write down a list of memory-jogger points that you hope to have covered during the interview and notes on information you need to remember after the interview.

These will include some or all of the following, plus anything else you think of that is important to you. List them on the left hand side of the page.

Name of your interviewer(s)

Their position in the company

Further company information (products/services)

The job description

Any training provided

Prospects

Salary/Holidays/Hours of work

What is the next step in the selection process

Anticipated starting date of successful candidate

TRAVEL

How are you getting there? If you are travelling to your interview by car, work out your route, or, if you are going by public transport look at relevant timetables. Know precisely which bus or train to catch. Know precisely when you need to leave home to arrive with time to spare. Have some suitable coins on you in case you have to phone the company if you are delayed on route.

CLOTHES

Decide what you are going to wear. Check your clothes over and make sure they are clean and well pressed. Clean shoes and fingernails are very important. Tip out your bag or case and get rid of the clutter. Wear an outfit that can be described as middle of the road — not too casual (jeans are not the thing) and not too flamboyant in colour or style. Go easy on the perfume or aftershave. Play safe but wear clothes you feel good in. As with application letters, your clothes, appearance and general tidiness say a lot about you and reflect your personality.

THINK OUT YOUR ANSWERS AND RESPONSES

You have given thought to the impression you wish to give and the questions you will be putting to your interviewer(s). But now think: 'What will they be trying to find out about me and what questions will they ask?'

Apart from a recognisable potential that they can identify on paper, with the specified qualifications and skills, they will also be looking for certain personal qualities that you possess. They will want to employ someone who is:

Responsible

Honest

Loyal

Hardworking

Who has acceptable social habits

Who will get on well with other members of staff

These are all important factors that contribute to your recognisable potential. In other words, someone who would prove an asset to the company and whom they could proudly introduce as a member of their staff.

Think about your answers to these examples of some typical questions and points of discussion. Be sure you are happy that they are honest answers.

What do you know about us?

Why are you interested in the job?

In what ways do you feel you are suitable for the job?

Do you think you can do the job?

Are you pleased with your examination results?

Why did you not do better in your examinations?

What are the most valuable benefits you have gained from University/ Polytechnic?

Have you made any decisions you regret in your academic career?

Have you responded well to the independence of University/Polytechnic life?

How do you get on with your contemporaries (classmates)?

Do you read a newspaper? Which one?

Why have you decided not to go on to further education?

How did you get on with your teachers/tutors?

How do you get on with your brothers/sisters at home?

What does your father/mother do for a living?

What are your career objectives?

What has been your greatest non-academic achievement?

Would you have time for further study in the evenings?

How would you travel to work if we offer you the job?

Are you a good timekeeper?

Do you think of yourself as a leader or a follower?

How do you like to spend your evenings?

How do you like to spend your weekends?

Talk about your leisure interests

Sum up your strengths

Sum up your weaknesses

Having run through these questions, you will no doubt find that you are not quite perfect so, in your conversation with your interviewer, highlight your strong points, your skills and good qualities and be reassured that no realistic manager is expecting to find total perfection in one human being.

A FEW MORE PRACTICAL TIPS

BUYING YOURSELF THINKING TIME

If you are asked a 'sticky' question, don't let your mind scramble — buy yourself some time by repeating the question. For instance:

Interviewer: What has been your greatest non-academic achievement?

Answer: What has been my greatest non-academic achievement? Oh Yes, it was when I won the . . .

You should only use this type of reply once, at the most twice, in the interview. Used more than that, it slows down the interview and your interviewer will get bored and perhaps irritated.

Another way of dealing with an awkward statement or question from the interviewer is to answer it with a question followed by a countering positive. For example, you are applying for a vacancy for an Accounts Clerk:

Interviewer: You achieved only a low grade for your Maths exam. Will your Maths stand up in this job?

Answer: Do you think it is likely to be a problem? I have cashiering experience from working at the Something Garage on Saturdays so I am not afraid of money and I do help my father with his bookkeeping sometimes.

Again, you should not reply in this manner more than once during the interview. Bear in mind, too, that it is a response that needs putting over in a friendly way. It must not sound challenging. It is useful only if it is done well.

'Yes' 'No' answers are absolutely fine but do try to follow them by a relevant remark, albeit a short one. For instance:

Interviewer: Would you have any problems getting here?

Answer: 'No.' I have checked. Numbers 87 and 54 buses are both on the right route and frequent. Either would get me here in plenty of time.

Sum up your strengths: Demonstrate those that are relevant to the job.
Sum up your weaknesses: Demonstrate those not relevant to the job.

ASSESSMENT TESTS

Designed to help and even fun to do, they are becoming increasingly used for recruitment purposes. If you are prepared for the possibility that they may come up during your interview, there is no reason why they should throw you off balance. It should be remembered that they are used to serve merely as an indicator to your suitability for the job.

There are various types of tests designed for different purposes.

SKILL TESTS: To demonstrate your level of ability in the skills you are offering, e.g. shorthand typing speeds.

APTITUDE TESTS: To measure potential suitability for a type of work, e.g. dexterity for assembly jobs.

KNOWLEDGE TESTS: To gain insight into general knowledge of candidate in subjects related to job.

INTELLIGENCE TESTS: To establish a candidate's power in reasoning and logic.

PERSONALITY TESTS: To gain insight into what makes an applicant tick — their motivations, strengths and weaknesses. Commonly used in recruiting graduates, management and sales staff.

ALL SET TO GO

You have your file or bag ready with everything you need for your interview in it. You know how you are travelling to your interview and what time you need to leave home. You know what you are going to wear and you have checked that your clothes are clean and well pressed. And you have thought out some answers to some likely questions. So now relax, get an early night, and wake up feeling positive and sharp-witted.

THE INTERVIEW

IT'S THE JOB YOU WANT — SO GO FOR IT!

You'll arrive for your interview a little before time feeling and looking relaxed and cool. More plus points chalked up before the interview has even started.

Take a deep breath and walk into their offices confidently — ready to clinch a job offer.

RELAX AND ENJOY YOURSELF

Think positive and not only want the job but intend to get the offer of it. You will be feeling nervous — and who wouldn't be in the situation? If you are afraid that your nerves will show, don't worry as you will find that you will relax increasingly as the interview progresses. An interview is an experience you should expect to enjoy.

A LITTLE BLUFF DOES NOT HURT

This is your chance to convince them of your interest and enthusiasm, ability and desire to do the job. A little bluff to demonstrate your self-confidence is not a bad thing as long as you do not overdo it. Modesty goes down better than arrogance and the line between confidence and arrogance is quite thin.

INTERVIEWS TAKE VARIOUS FORMS

THE ONE TO ONE

These are usually formal in-depth interviews in which you will meet your interviewers one at a time. Typically, you will be interviewed by a Personnel Officer or Manager and then go on to an interview with the Manager of the 'user' department, or sometimes vice versa. If you are lucky you will have both interviews on the same day but there are occasions when you will be invited to return for the second interview.

INTERVIEW PANEL

These are a meeting with several interviewers in the room who will usually take turns in asking you questions. This type of interview can be rather daunting at first sight. However, you will get used to it after a few minutes, once you have taken in the faces of those on the panel and exchanged a few pleasantries with them. They are formal in-depth interviews, when you should make a point of addressing your answer to the member of the panel that puts the question to you by looking at him or her whilst acknowledging the other members at the end of your answer.

GROUP INTERVIEWS

These take the form of a debate with other candidates. You will be given a topic to discuss and your communication ability, behaviour and contribution will be assessed by a company observer.

'WALK IN' INTERVIEWS

These can be fun if you are prepared to be patient. They are usually staged off the company premises at a hotel or the like. The 'just turn up' approach is used to speed up the recruitment process and attract a greater number of applicants. Companies find them useful when they have several jobs to fill. They are informal, relaxed occasions where you will be saturated with information and coffee but it may be a while before you meet your interviewer. You will have a short interview and, if you express interest in the position, you will either be given an application form or you may be booked in on the spot for a formal interview on the company premises.

SUM UP YOUR INTERVIEWER

Think of an interview as a two-way exchange of information for the purpose of establishing whether you are right for the job and the job is right for you.

YOU ARE THERE TO LEARN ABOUT THE COMPANY TOO.

Every interviewer has his or her own 'style' and it is worth bearing in mind that some interviewers are more experienced than others. Quite often you will find that the least experienced among them will conduct the least formal interviews. This may sound fine but be careful. He or she can mislead you unintentionally by their apparent enthusiasm at the interview, only to disappoint you later. The more experienced are masters at giving little away, so when you leave they will have given you few or no clues as to your chances. They are consciously keeping an open mind until they have seen everyone. Whatever form the interview takes and in whatever style it is conducted, the object of the exercise is to employ the right person for the job.

At the end of the interview you will expect to have been told all that is necessary about the company and the job to make your decisions about them and, for the interviewer's part, they will expect you to have been as open about yourself in order that they can make their decision about you.

MORE INTERVIEW TIPS

YOUR ENTRANCE

Report to Reception and give them your name, the name of the person you are seeing and the appointment time.

While you are waiting, sit down if invited, and take in your surroundings. Have a quick scan through any company literature that might be lying on the table in the reception area.

When your interviewer or his or her secretary comes to meet you, stand up when they walk over to you and be ready to shake hands. Let them extend their hand first. Ask if you should take your coat with you or if there is anywhere they would like you to leave it.

THE INTERVIEW SESSION

Once you have entered the interview room, sit down only when you are invited to do so.

If you are introduced to several interviewers, try to remember their names and their job titles. Smile while the introductions are being made. You probably will find that one person makes a point of coming forward to you. They will make the introductions and will indicate a chair for you to sit down on. Sit straight or slightly inclined forward.

Sit tidily. Put your file on your lap. Do not put anything down on the interviewer's desk — that's their territory. Don't encroach on it unless you are invited to do so.

Pull out from your file your CV and notes.

If you are asked if you would like a cup of something, accept if you would like one and answer 'Yes Please, if it's no bother'. If your nerves are making you feel awkward and a bit clumsy, it is better to say 'No, thank you'. Cups can be difficult to handle when you have a lap full of file.

Take note of your surroundings but keep awake and concentrate on what is being said. Do not be distracted by your interviewer's face or mannerisms. And remember to control your own movements. Do not fiddle with jewellery or clothing.

Do not avoid eye contact — a little sparkle can work wonders. It relaxes interviewers as well.

If you are asked if you would like a cigarette, say thanks but always decline the offer.

When you get on to the subject of qualifications, ask if they would like to see your certificates.

If the interview is interrupted by someone coming into the room or a telephone call being put through to your interviewer, show how patient and discreet you can be. Use the time, not to earwig but to look around you and take in the office. Don't sigh, stretch or look bored. The interviewer will be irritated at the interruption but will notice if you react well when the unexpected happens.

Be aware of the signals to leave. It may be that your interviewer will put down their pen and tidy up papers that relate to the interview. They may lean back in their chair. They may look at their watch.

Their closing phrases are likely to be: 'Do you have any further questions for me?' 'Thank you for coming to see me today.' 'We will be in contact . . .' Taking these as closing questions, statements and actions, prepare to take your leave. Do not try to prolong the interview. Thank the interviewer for the interview and part on the note that you have found the interview very interesting and that it is a job you would like to do.

YOUR EXIT

Leave the interview room as tidily and confidently as you came in. Take all your belongings with you.

Once you have left the interview room, try to orientate yourself again so you set off down the corridor in the right direction. If you can't remember, simply ask 'How do I find my way back to Reception?' It's better than losing yourself and feeling silly.

Under no circumstances go back to the interview room after you have left it. If you suddenly realise that you have left something in there, always ask a secretary or the receptionist to retrieve it for you.

Say goodbye to the secretary who might show you out and thank her. Say goodbye to the receptionist when you pass, if she is free. Be pleasant to everyone so they all feel that you are a nice person to have around.

STEP 5
AFTER THE INTERVIEW

As soon as possible after an interview, complete your interview notes on everything you know about the job and company. Put down all the pros and cons, so that, if you are offered the job, you can see whether it's one that matches your requirements and if there are any queries that you may need to put to the company before making your decision.

If it's a job that really appeals to you, a short letter to your interviewer at the company thanking them for the interview and confirming your interest in the position is a good idea. It should run along these lines:

1, Valley Green,
Strentham,
Bucks BU10 9LJ

8 June, 1989

Mr. R. Fisher,
Cam Engineering Ltd.,
Viking Way,
Hornfield,
Bucks BU15 6QL

Dear Mr. Fisher,

Re: Your vacancy for an Accounts Assistant

I write to thank you for seeing me on 6 June.
I enjoyed my interview very much and I would like to confirm my interest in the job.
It is work that I feel I could do well and I look forward to hearing from you again soon.

Yours sincerely,

JOHN SMITH

WHAT NEXT?

You are not home and dry yet . . .

The answer, even if you have left an interview convinced of your success and 100 per cent sure that you would like the job, is to keep looking and applying for other vacancies. Keep yourself in a job-hunting routine and do not relax your efforts until you have a watertight offer in writing, spelling out conditions of employment and salary. Even in the most certain of cases, things can go wrong. Once you have called a halt to the search, it is difficult to find the energy to start all over again. *So keep going*. Hopefully, at the end of the day you will have a choice of offers.

PROBLEMS

Taking 'No' for an answer — is it you, or just bad luck?

Unfortunately, you have to expect some turndowns and silences from companies. Taking 'No' for an answer is always hard but you have to be prepared for some negative outcomes, particularly if you have tried the speculative approach with your applications. With these, to a great extent, it is the luck of the draw. The right job being available at the right time for you is a matter of luck. However, if after a reasonable time and a number of applications you are receiving only rejections, there must come a point when you have to ask yourself 'Why?' The questions that should be considered are:

Am I applying for the wrong jobs?

Am I approaching my applications somehow wrongly?

Could my C.V. be improved?

Am I projecting myself badly on interview?

Having asked yourself these questions and perhaps not coming up with any particularly useful answers, you should talk it through with other people whose opinions you respect. The most obvious will be your career advisers but the views of family and friends can be very helpful too. It may be they feel that you are doing all the right things and it is just a matter of bad luck so, if you continue as you are, the right offer will come up for you before long.

A JOB OFFER

So this is what it's all been about. An offer on your doormat. You should expect the letter to include information on the following:

Your job title

Your hours of work

Your holiday entitlement

Your salary and review periods

The length of notice you have to give them should you wish to leave

The length of notice they have to give you

Read it carefully and make sure you understand every point.

Alternatively, it may be a brief letter with a Terms and Conditions of Employment enclosed providing all the statutory information that is required to be given within the first 13 weeks of your employment. However, to make a decision as to whether or not to take the job you need the above information at the very least.

Assuming you are happy, write to the company as soon as possible giving your acceptance. As insurance, it is also a good idea to ring them and let them know that your acceptance is in the post. A letter of acceptance could be along these lines:

1, Valley Green,
Strentham,
Bucks BU10 9LJ

8 June, 1989

Mr. R. Fisher,
Cam Engineering Ltd.,
Viking Way,
Hornfield
Bucks BU15 6QL

Dear Mr. Fisher,

Re: Your vacancy for an Accounts Assistant.

   I write to thank you for your letter of 12 June offering me the position of Accounts Assistant.
   I am pleased to accept your offer and I look forward to starting work with you on 2 July 1989.

Yours sincerely,

JOHN SMITH

Always keep the offer letter safe and keep a copy of your acceptance.
   Having accepted a job it is very important to cancel any outstanding appointments for interviews with other companies. Do not forget in the excitement of your success.

CONCLUSION

YOU HAVE TO PLAY TO WIN IF YOU ARE TO GET ANYWHERE.

I hope the information in this book has gone some way to providing a step-by-step help while you are job hunting and that you will soon have a job to look forward to starting.

You will succeed by identifying your skills and qualities and matching them to the opportunities right for you. You must be determined and organised and market your potential in the right way. If you do all of this, then . . .

YOU DESERVE TO BE A WINNER!

NOTES

NOTES